CW00338110

Gospel Classi...

Arranged by Mark Hayes

12 Artistic Arrangements for Worship Services, Concerts and Recitals

From my first memories as a child to my present career as a composer and arranger, hymns and gospel songs have been an important piece in the musical fabric of my life. I started playing piano for congregational worship when I was 13 years old. During my high school years, I sang in the church choir. While at college, I learned to arrange hymns for various choral groups. Shortly after graduation, my first collection of solo piano arrangements for church pianists was published, fulfilling a dream of mine.

During devotional times, favorite old hymns are often what I play at the piano. As an arranger, I look for ways to breathe new life into old gospel songs. As a worship leader, I receive immense satisfaction when I see worshipers respond to a new setting of an old hymn and experience its timeless truth in a fresh way.

Despite the changes in worship that are occurring in churches all over the world, hymns and gospel songs—the music of our faith traditions—are alive and well and still very important to us. These old melodies and messages connect with us on a deeply emotional and spiritual level. They feed and nourish our souls.

To that end, I am pleased to present this collection of classic hymns and gospel songs—my first piano collection with Alfred Music Publishing. It's always a challenge for me to find the "heart" of a song and express that in my own unique way. You'll find these arrangements to be joyous, reflective, passionate and playful. May they delight your ears, stir your spirit, and feed your soul.

Mark Hayes

A CD recording of the selections contained in this book, performed by Mark Hayes, is available.

Copyright © MMIII by Alfred Music Publishing Co., Inc.
All rights reserved.   Printed in U.S.A.
ISBN 0-7390-3104-X (Book)
ISBN 0-7390-3105-8 (Book and CD)

Performance Notes

Sweet By and By 3

The concept of heaven probably means something different to every person. In this musical representation, I've tried to created a state of peace and tranquility through the lushness of the chords and the unhurried, undulating rhythm of the eighth-note patterns. At measure 29, the time signature switches to $\frac{3}{4}$, which provides an almost lilting quality. The coda at measure 105 returns to a dreamlike, almost celestial state, with a simple ascending melody taking us to higher realms.

He Hideth My Soul 8

The initial mood of this arrangement is one of delicacy and simplicity. Find a tempo that allows you to play the 16th-note passages easily and unhurried. Take time to read the text (p. 64) of this hymn, especially noting the joyous lift in the last verse so you may communicate that to your listener. The 32d notes in measure 56 fit easily under the hand. In order to achieve greater clarity, try raising your fingers a bit more when playing this passage, even though it's fast.

When I Can Read My Title Clear . . . 12

This hymn tune lends itself to a contemporary, rhythmic treatment that expresses the joy and eagerness with which we look forward to heaven. The left-hand pattern almost sounds like a drum cadence. Rhythmic stability is crucial here. Pay careful attention to the staccato articulations and use the damper pedal sparingly.

Heavenly Sunlight 16

If ever there were a gospel song that is full of joy and happiness, this is it. As I set out to arrange this piece, I decided to give it a "happy" shuffle feel in $\frac{4}{4}$ time, as opposed to its original $\frac{9}{8}$ time signature. Keep it light and jazzy. Take care to emphasize the melody, which is usually in the top voice of the right hand, except at measures 38–51. In this left-hand melody section, tenutos indicate the melody. As with any rhythmic and syncopated piece, it's crucial to keep a steady tempo.

I Will Arise and Go to Jesus 22

This haunting melody lends itself particularly well to a more romantic feel. The motive at the beginning is almost Chopinesque. Notice the tempo changes throughout. Play the section at measure 30 deliberately and passionately.

In the Garden 26

The introduction of this old gospel song is meditative, and has the intentional sound of Erik Satie's *Gymnopédies*. I've written this arrangement in $\frac{3}{4}$ instead of $\frac{6}{8}$ to make it easier to read, but don't be in too much of a hurry. Play it with a languid feel where appropriate. Feel free to move ahead in more of a waltz tempo at measures 60 and 83, then return to the original tempo at measure 105. You're walking in the garden, with all the time in the world.

I'll Fly Away 31

I'm not sure how I got the idea to set this great old gospel song in a quasi-ragtime* style, but I think it fits perfectly! The first statement is reflective and needs time for the "color" chords to resonate. Once you reach measure 17, cut loose and have fun! Keep a steady tempo. Because of the inner voices, take extra care to project the melody throughout. The stride pattern in the left hand is a prominent characteristic of ragtime and can be challenging. I would suggest some "left hand only" practice until you can be consistently accurate with all those leaps.

(Performance Notes continue on page 63)

---

* Authentic ragtime is played with even eighth notes; however, I chose to "swing" the eighths for a jazzier feel.

Sweet By and By

Joseph P. Webster
Arr. Mark Hayes

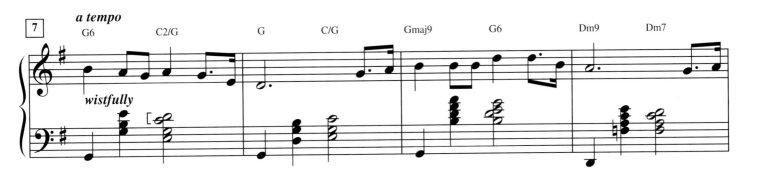

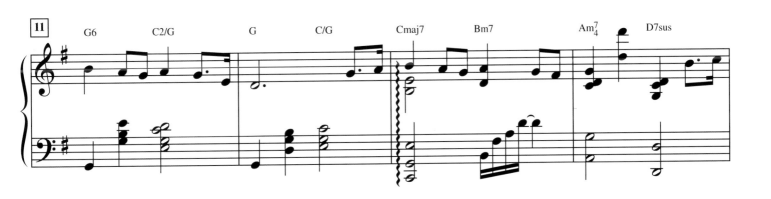

To the glory of God, in honor of Diane Ford,
for 25 years of sharing God's gift of music with First Baptist Church, Radford, Virginia

HE HIDETH MY SOUL

William J. Kirkpatrick
Arr. Mark Hayes

WHEN I CAN READ MY TITLE CLEAR

Scottish Melody
Arr. Mark Hayes

HEAVENLY SUNLIGHT

George Harrison Cook
Arr. Mark Hayes

I Will Arise and Go to Jesus

Southern Folk Melody
Arr. Mark Hayes

In the Garden

C. Austin Miles
Arr. Mark Hayes

I'll Fly Away

Albert E. Brumley
Arr. Mark Hayes

There Is a Balm in Gilead

Spiritual
Arr. Mark Hayes

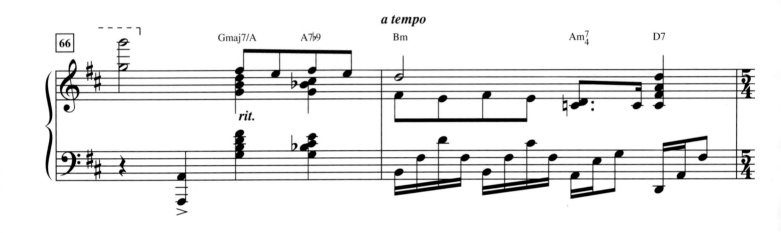

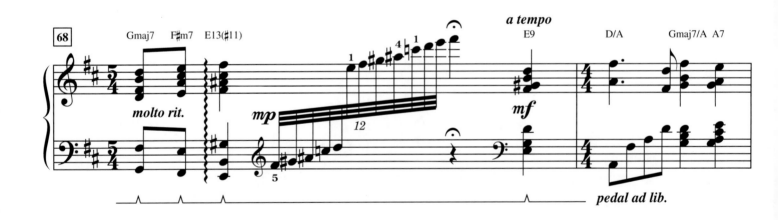

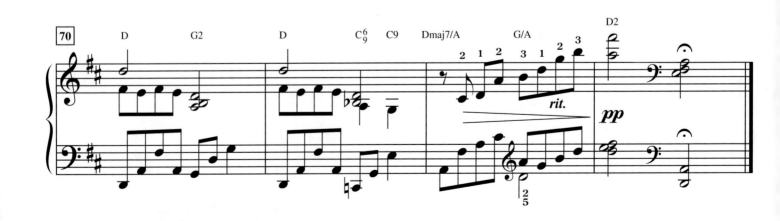

When the Roll Is Called Up Yonder

James M. Black
Arr. Mark Hayes

When We All Get to Heaven—Emily D. Wilson

ON JORDAN'S STORMY BANKS

M. Durham
Arr. Mark Hayes

THE OLD RUGGED CROSS

George Bennard
Arr. Mark Hayes

How Great Thou Art

Words and Music by Stuart K. Hine
Arr. Mark Hayes

Performance Notes *(continued from page 2)*

There Is a Balm in Gilead 36

Many gospel songs and spirituals speak of the life hereafter. Gilead, a historic place in biblical times, is also a metaphor for the afterlife—a place where we will be made whole. My design for this song was to create a mood of peace and tranquility, a musical place that would feel soothing and nurturing. Make the descending-sixth passages in measures 1–6 and 35–41 as flowing and connected as possible. Enjoy the warmth of the key of D-flat at measure 42.

When the Roll Is Called Up Yonder 41

If I were playing this arrangement with a live rhythm section, I would tell the players to play in a Latin, almost samba style. Ever since I visited Brazil, I've looked for ways to use those wonderful Brazilian rhythms and jazz harmonies in my music. This arrangement quotes an extra hymn, *When We All Get to Heaven,* tucked away in the middle of the piece. Play with exuberance and enjoy the contemporary edge!

On Jordan's Stormy Banks 47

I have arranged this hymn tune in a syncopated pop style to highlight the excitement and anticipation of the Promised Land inherent in the text. The most important thing to do when playing this piece is to keep a steady tempo. Whenever music is syncopated, it requires a consistent, steady beat so the syncopations can be played without rushing. Enjoy the reharmonizations of the melody.

The Old Rugged Cross 51

Although this hymn is a sentimental favorite of many, the subject of the cross is far from pleasant. As I read through this hymn text, I opted to set the first two verses in a minor key to underscore the agony of the cross. This arrangement starts in the style of the great romantics, like Rachmaninoff, and needs to be played with great passion as well as nuance throughout. I wrote in an orchestral fashion, using the full range of the piano. When the key center shifts to C major at measure 82, it comes as a welcome relief, partly because of the heaviness of the minor sound that precedes it. Linger at that transition before moving into the major key. Take time to read the fourth stanza of the hymn text before you play this final verse. It speaks of the joy that awaits us in heaven. Let the dissonance sink in at measures 121–122 before the resolution to the final C-major chord.

How Great Thou Art 56

This piece is definitely the "tour de force" of the collection; consequently, it is the most technically demanding piece to play. I've attempted to capture some of the grandness of God in this arrangement and crafted it in an intentionally orchestral style. For those of you who can't play repeated octaves comfortably, feel free to leave out some notes. For instance, in measures 1–3, you could play the right hand as single notes instead of octaves. The passage in measures 6–7 is simply a repetition of broken D-flat and E-flat chords. To practice, try playing each group of 32d notes as a block chord, in order to master each inversion. It's very important to take time with the various moods within this piece. Read the hymn text and pay careful attention to how it is painted through the music. You may play this piece as slowly as needed in order to perform it artistically, capturing the grandeur of this beloved hymn.

About the Chord Symbols

Chord symbols have been added to each arrangement to help people who play by chord as well as by notes, to educate budding arrangers in naming new harmonies, and to encourage pianists in the art of improvisation.

Note: Some chord symbols utilizing the slash mark may indicate inversions that are different from the written notes, especially in some left-hand chords. In those cases, the chord symbols reflect "implied" harmonies, indicating notes that a bass guitarist or other similar instrumentalist might play.

Sweet By and By
Words: Sanford F. Bennett, 1836–1898
Music: Joseph P. Webster, 1819–1875

There's a land that is fairer than day,
  and by faith we can see it afar;
For the Father waits over the way
  to prepare us a dwelling place there.

We shall sing on that beautiful shore
  the melodious songs of the blest,
And our spirits shall sorrow no more,
  not a sigh for the blessing of rest.

To our bountiful Father above,
  we will offer the tribute of praise
For the glorious gift of His love
  and the blessings that hallow our days.

Refrain:
In the sweet by and by, we shall meet on that beautiful shore;
In the sweet by and by, we shall meet on that beautiful shore.

He Hideth My Soul
Words: Fanny J. Crosby, 1820–1915
Music: William J. Kirkpatrick, 1838–1921

A wonderful Savior is Jesus my Lord,
A wonderful Savior to me;
He hideth my soul in the cleft of the rock,
Where rivers of pleasure I see.

A wonderful Savior is Jesus my Lord,
He taketh my burden away;
He holdeth me up, and I shall not be moved,
He giveth me strength as my day.

With numberless blessings each moment He crowns,
And filled with His fullness divine,
I sing in my rapture, oh, glory to God
For such a Redeemer as mine!

When clothed in His brightness, transported I rise
To meet Him in clouds of the sky,
His perfect salvation, His wonderful love
I'll shout with the millions on high.

Refrain:
He hideth my soul in the cleft of the rock
That shadows a dry, thirsty land;
He hideth my life in the depths of His love,
And covers me there with His hand,
And covers me there with His hand.

When I Can Read My Title Clear
Words: Isaac Watts, 1674–1748
Music: Scottish Melody

When I can read my title clear to mansions in the skies,
I'll bid farewell to every fear, and wipe my weeping eyes;
And wipe my weeping eyes, and wipe my weeping eyes,
I'll bid farewell to every fear, and wipe my weeping eyes.

Should earth against my soul engage, and fiery darts be hurled,
Then I can smile at Satan's rage, and face a frowning world;
And face a frowning world, and face a frowning world,
Then I can smile at Satan's rage, and face a frowning world.

Let cares, like a wild deluge come, and storms of sorrow fall!
May I but safely reach my home, my God, my heaven, my all;
My God, my heaven, my all, my God, my heaven, my all,
May I but safely reach my home, my God, my heaven, my all.

There shall I bathe my weary soul in seas of heavenly rest,
And not a wave of trouble roll across my peaceful breast;
Across my peaceful breast, across my peaceful breast,
And not a wave of trouble roll across my peaceful breast.

Heavenly Sunlight
Words: Henry J. Zelley, 1859–1942
Music: George Harrison Cook, ?–1948

Walking in sunlight, all of my journey;
Over the mountains, thro' the deep vale;
Jesus has said "I'll never forsake Thee,"
Promise divine that never can fail.

Shadows around me, shadows above me,
Never conceal my Savior and Guide;
He is the light, in Him is no darkness;
Ever I'm walking close to His side.

In the bright sunlight, ever rejoicing,
Pressing my way to mansions above;
Singing His praises gladly I'm walking,
Walking in sunlight, sunlight of love.

Refrain:
Heavenly sunlight, heavenly sunlight,
Flooding my soul with glory divine;
Hallelujah, I am rejoicing,
Singing His praises, Jesus is mine.

I Will Arise and Go to Jesus
Words: Joseph Hart (refrain anonymous)
Music: Southern Folk Melody

Come, ye sinners, poor and needy,
Weak and wounded, sick and sore;
Jesus ready stands to save you,
Full of pity, love and power.

Come, ye thirsty, come, and welcome,
God's free bounty glorify;
True belief and true repentance,
Every grace that brings you nigh.

Come, ye weary, heavy-laden,
Lost and ruined by the fall;
If you tarry till you're better,
You will never come at all.

Refrain:
I will arise and go to Jesus,
He will embrace me in His arms.
In the arms of my dear Savior,
Oh, there are ten thousand charms.

In the Garden
Words & Music by C. Austin Miles, 1868–1946

I come to the garden alone
  while the dew is still on the roses;
And the voice I hear falling on my ear,
  the Son of God discloses.

He speaks, and the sound of His voice
  is so sweet, the birds hush their singing;
And the melody that He gave to me
  within my heart is ringing.

I'd stay in the garden with Him
  though the night around me be falling,
But He bids me go, through the voice of woe,
  His voice to me is calling.

Refrain:
And He walks with me, and He talks with me,
And He tells me I am His own.
And the joy we share as we tarry there,
None other has ever known.